Enochian Walks with God

Walk Like Enoch Walked, Talk Like
Enoch Talked, Go Where Enoch Went

Russell Walden
www.fathersheartministry.net

Chapter One

Which Enoch are You?

Introduction: Which Enoch are You?

In our study here, we are going to consider the life and testimony of a man by the name of Enoch. He is unique in the annals of spiritual history being the first of two men (not even Jesus) who returned to the Father, but not by way of the grave. In our study by the grace of God, we will consider just what translation is and answer the question, "is it still available to us" individually today? In other words, "can I experience what

Enoch experienced in my own life in Christ or do

I have to wait for the rapture?" We will also bring understanding about how to walk like Enoch walked, talk like Enoch talked, and go where Enoch went (and are you sure you want to?).

In studying Enoch, it would be easy to jump right onto the revelatory bandwagon and wow you with some deep truths that will provoke you to buy every book on our book table. However, I don't want to circumvent your heart before dazzling your mind with my scintillating revelation (tongue firmly in cheek here). We know very little of Enoch's thinking and philosophy. It isn't Enoch's mind that captivates us or distinguished him among men. What made Enoch different was his heart and his faith. Enoch's faith was an intimate thing that consumed his entire being until the point that there was nothing left to him as a man, or nothing left for him to do, but to look to the Lord and be dismissed in a blaze of glory.

So we begin by looking at the character of Enoch and the contrast of the Enoch of Genesis 5:24 and the Enoch – the first born Enoch who was not a godly man, but was actually the first born son in the line of Cain.

Where the Title Comes From:

The title, "Enochian Walks with God", is actually borrowed from the writings of a 17th-century Christian mystic by the name of Jane Leade. Jane came from an affluent family in Norfolk, England and lived a conventional happily married to a businessman and merchant for 27 years. After her husband's death, she experienced a vision that changed her life forever and resulted in her name being known to us for the remarkable piety and depth of spirituality she walked in.

In Jane's first writings, she saw the paradise of God as something that existed on the inside of her own person. Her understanding was that whatever Eden was – that the tree of life was something sought after inwardly and found upon the opening of an inward and divine door that changed her life forever. This agrees with the writings of Paul who declared in Col. 1:27 that the mystery hidden from ages and generations is now made manifest to the saints which was: "Christ in you the hope of glory…" Paul goes on in v. 28-29 to specify that this message of Christ in you was the message for which he was contending and "warning every man, and teaching every man" in the hopes that we might be presented "complete in Christ".

What is the warning? When we are found looking outwardly to Christian culture for what we should be seeking for inwardly, then those who operate in the spirit and apostleship of Paul are standing in our way pointing back to who Christ is IN YOU and not the false dependencies of religious intuitions or Christian cultural misdirection.

Who Was Enoch?

There are two Enochs in scripture – one was a descendant of Cain and the other an ancestor of Noah. Enoch's name means "dedicated and consecrated" (coincidentally the name of Enoch is also where the word Hannukah originates). The one Enoch was of the line of Cain and dedicated to his own way and his own destruction. The other Enoch was dedicated to God and was not for God took him.

So we see that there are two Enochs in the earth. There are two men or companies of men in the earth and they are both in pursuit of what they worship. There are two natures at work on the inside of us and the end result will be the same:

[Gen 5:24 KJV] 24 And Enoch walked with God: and he [was] not; for God took him.

We look at this verse, and if you have any love for God, we declare, "that is what I want!" I want to walk with God and be captivated and lost in Him. We have to pause, however, and know that there is an Enoch in every one of us – even the unregenerate. That is the message of two Enochs, one in the line of Cain and the other in the line of Seth. Jesus said no man can serve to masters. At every moment of every day of your existence, you are in pursuit of one or the other. You are either pursuing the god of the line of Cain or pursuing the God of the line of Noah. That pursuit will also irrevocably and unavoidably have an end result of which we see the positive in Gen. 5:24. One day every man walking with his god will be not, for his "god" or his "God" will take him. The question is the character of that pursuit. What god are you in pursuit of?

The Other Enoch:

In Genesis 4:16-17, we find that Enoch was Cain's firstborn after he went out from the presence of

God. We don't just wander out of the presence of God. Finding ourselves outside of the presence of God is not just happenstance; it is a pursuit in us without respect to the consequences. Enoch was Cain's firstborn, and after his birth, Cain built and named a city after his son. Now think of it. Cain is a murderer and is expelled from God's presence. What does he do? Does he live in contrition and repentance? No, he goes out and establishes a city and a culture of godlessness, having gone OUT from the presence of God. He names his son and his city "dedicated and consecrated". Consecrated to what? Not consecrated to God. He wasn't trying to make up with the God that he had offended. What was the dedication and consecration of Cain that his first born son's name and the name of his city represented?

Why did Cain murder Abel? Because he was walking in self-referral rather than God consciousness. The brothers made sacrifice to God and Cain didn't like what Abel's sacrifice made him look like. Abel brought sacrificial blood in a covenantal transaction. Cain just brought the works of his hands expecting God to take what he had to offer. The city Cain built was populated by those with a performance-based approach to life that says, "I will put forth the effort and I expect life to render to me my just due…"

How many times do we think like this? "I've paid my dues!" I don't deserve this! And like Cain, we build around us a circle of friends and a culture of self-justification that excuses our offenses against God and justifies us, not on the basis of sacrificial blood and covenantal transaction, but rather justifies our existence on the basis of comparison with others and our own performance-based thinking. This approach to life and the meaning of life can become a lifelong obsession that will consume you until there is nothing left. It promises you attainment and accomplishment, but in the end, like the second Enoch, you will walk in that path and "be not" for what you pursue will "take you", and the end result for the first Enoch will not be as the blessed outcome for the second Enoch.

What Kind of Enoch are You?

Which Enoch are you? Every man has both Enochs on the inside of him. Which one you are is betrayed in the pursuit you are engaged in. Are you pursuing self-referral, materialism, notoriety or fame? Or are you in pursuit of an end all abandonment to who Christ died to be on the inside of you?

What is the determination of your heart today in regard to walking with God? Is Jesus an accouterment to your life enhancing and garnishing a life of self-determinism and personal agendas? Is He a little dashboard Jesus or a bobble head Jesus as your go merrily on your way leaning full tilt into your own purposes, plans and pursuits? God is interested in more than dousing you with the "magic touch" of Charismatic, Pentecostal Christianity. He didn't call us merely to be converted and just salt our life of self-referral with a little "Jesus" when necessary. Jesus came to earth seeking out not just those willing to make a crisis decision to accept him as savior, but those rather that are willing to become immersed in a divine pursuit in a process called discipleship that will last your whole life long.

Now I am after you on this one now. There is deep and revelatory truth in the understanding of Enoch; who he was, where he went and what it means to you and me. I want, however, not just to give you a bowl of revelatory ice cream that you can say "oooooh, isn't that great" and "didn't you enjoy that"? I want to take you through the truths of Enoch and deposit you behind the veil and see you begin to experience what it is to be changed men and changed women who are ruined for the kingdom and having the trajectory of your life forever altered by the visage of Christ unveiled before you in the testimony of a man called Enoch.

Conclusion:

In her earliest writings Jane Leade penned these words that I will paraphrase here:

> *For there is a Center Deeper still, where God is transparently revealed beyond any need of image or similitude or metaphor. There is a center in yourself beyond a door marked "Deeper Still" where God is known by you and seen in his own Simplified Being. In Spirit caught up here there is brought forth in us the very essential properties of the life of God wrought out of the immediacy of His presence IN us and AROUND us whereby we are replenished in vision and brought to the Habitation of God where we know with all the delightful Satisfaction, what the very Angels before the Throne of God's Majesty do enjoy.*

Before a step further in enlightening the mind regarding Enoch we want to pause here and turn your heart to a place of being fully attuned to the inner life – the inner universe on the inside of you where God finds his space and establishes in you the transformative reality that Paul spoke of as "Christ in You the Hope of Glory".

Chapter Two

Enoch's Appointment with Death is Cancelled

Introduction: Enoch's Appointment with Death is Cancelled

In part one of our study on Enoch, we looked at the two men by that name in the scripture. The first Enoch was the first born son of Cain. The second Enoch was the seventh from Adam. Both

of these names mean "dedicated, consecrated..."
In studying the implications of having two
Enochs, we are reminded of Augustine's "City of
God" which was written after the fall of the
Roman Empire. The reason Augustine wrote
"City of God" was to answer the accusation of
the pagans of his day that Rome fell because it
embraced Christianity. In this writing, Augustine
proposed that there were two cities in the earth –
one built on love of self and the other built on
love of God. We see this theme reflected in the
scriptures that give a record of not one but two
Enochs.

The question in this inquiry is which Enoch are
you? The Enoch from the line of Cain was
dedicated to himself and to the legacy of Cain.
The Enoch of Gen. 5:24 dedicated and
consecrated himself to God. Inside every one of
us, we can find both Enochs. Both of them are
dedicated and consecrated to a walk. One walks
after self-love and one walks after the love of
God. The first Enoch's father (Cain) built a city
and named it after him. Enoch was never known
to build a city, but his descendant Abraham had a
testimony that he sought a city whose builder
and maker is God (Hebrews 11:10).

In this study, we will look further into the heart
of Enoch the seventh from Adam.

Who Was Enoch?

Enoch was born in the line of Adam's third son Seth. His father was Jared and Enoch himself was the father of Methuselah. It is interesting that in these two men we find the shortest and the longest lifespan of the antediluvian patriarchs. In his lineage, Enoch was the seventh of the line of ten Patriarchs who were born and lived out their lives on the other side of the flood. The idea from folklore of the seventh son comes from the unique life and subsequent translation of Enoch in Gen. 5:24. Enoch was a seventh son and his son Methuselah was the son of a seventh son.

The Bible does not bear out any mystical or special standing of a seventh son, but it is interesting to note that Len Dawson, who led the Kansas City Chiefs to a Super Bowl victory, was the son of a seventh son. Singer Perry Como also held the distinction of being a seventh son. The number seven is the number of days that God used to form the earth and rest on the Sabbath. The etymology of the number seven speaks of covenant meaning "to cut". The Hebrew glyph of the number speaks to us of a crowned man. Other ancient glyphs of the number seven come from a pictogram of a kneeling man. For Enoch to be the seventh from Adam and to be the only man other than Elijah to be translated directly to heaven is not without significance.

The translation of Enoch is surrounded in mysticism and has been for centuries. Most mystic traditions hold that Enoch was translated because of secret knowledge or gnostic insights gained in his lifetime. In other words, the inference is that Enoch gained translation because he attained to some mystic state. The fact that he is also connected with the number seven belies that supposition. The number seven meaning "to cut" or being connected with the idea of covenant tells us that it is not Enoch's mysticism that resulted in his translation but rather his relationship with God. This is very important to note because, in the matter of Cain and Abel, Cain was rejected because he approached God with the works of his hands (Gen. 4:3). Abel, on the other hand, brought sacrificial blood in a covenantal transaction and was accepted (Gen. 4:4). If we are going to come to God like Enoch came to God it will be after the testimony of Enoch's ancestor Abel. The writer of Hebrews confirms this:

> *[Heb. 10:19-20 KJV] 19 Having therefore,*

> *brethren, boldness to enter into the holiest by the blood of Jesus, 20 By a new and living way, which he hath consecrated for us, through the veil, that is to say, his flesh;*

The way into the Holiest or the Holy of Holies is open. It is because of the shed blood of Jesus in a covenantal transaction between God and man that we come to God. The way is made clear for us not by our mysticism or religious performance. It is not some consecration on our part that we presume to follow Enoch's example but rather we recognize by faith that it is the consecration of Jesus produced in us that brings us through the veil of our sinful flesh by the same divine process that he stepped through the veil of his sinless flesh.

Is There Significance in the Number of Years Enoch Lived?

If Enoch walked with God, we can only assume that it was not something that he came late to in life. The patriarchs were extremely long lived before the flood. There are many reasons speculated as to why this is so, but we cannot ignore that Enoch came of age as we do today and lived an adult life for over three centuries. His walk with God was long, yet God no doubt chose his 365th year as the year of his translation. Because his translation was a matter of covenantal grace and not mystical attainment there is an implied meaning then that we can find out that it was in the 365th year of his life.

Obviously, 365 is the number of days in the year of the Gregorian calendar. The number 365 is interesting mathematically and it is interesting that a year with 365 days comes from a solar calendar and not a lunar calendar. In Judaism, there are 365 "abstain" or negative commandments (corresponding to the solar year) and 248 positive commandments (a number ascribed to the sum of the number of bones and major organs in the human body). Some Gnostic traditions held that there were 365 levels of heaven. The sum of all numbers with multiples of six mentioned in the Bible total 365. Six is the number of man. Therefore, the number 365 points to man's humanity in relationship with God. In other words, Enoch's life was a very human life. He was not a demigod as some ancient texts suggest, and while his experience of translation is unique, Enoch in himself was not a uniquely pious man whose sanctity somehow earned him translation. This is implied as well in the life of Elijah who also was translated:

> *[Jas 5:17 KJV] 17 Elias was a man subject to like passions as we are, and he prayed earnestly that it might not rain: and it rained not on the earth by the space of three years and six months.*

In other words, the men who were translated (Enoch and Elijah) are not set aside in scripture as unique in the sense that they earn or attained translation in a manner that is not accessible to men of "like passion" as we ourselves are. Whatever the message of Enoch's life and translation is – it is not the message of an experience and walk with God unattainable to you and me.

365 "Fear Nots" In the Bible:

Lastly, in Christianity, there are 365 "fear not" scriptures in the Bible. How is that significant and what is the connection with Enoch and his lifespan? Enoch (obviously) did not see death. He was translated in his 365th year. Now scholars today scoff at the idea that men lived to advanced ages mentioned before the flood. They speculate that these exaggerated lifespans were a literary artifice that cites these extended years for a rhetorical or symbolic meaning. Nonetheless, for Enoch to live 365 years and for this correspond to the number of "fear not" verses in the Bible brings us to the following verse:

> *[Heb 2:14-15 KJV] 14 Forasmuch then as the children are partakers of flesh and blood, he also himself likewise took part of the same; that through death he might destroy him that had the power of death, that is, the devil; 15 And deliver them who through fear of death were all their lifetime subject to bondage.*

Death had no power on Enoch. If, as the scriptures say, it is appointed unto man once to die (Heb. 9:27) – then Enoch's appointment was cancelled. We can cancel a dentist's appointment but God can cancel your appointment with death and did so for two men in the scripture (Enoch and Elijah). All fear exists and arises from a fear of death. Death is not your friend. Death is the last enemy of God (1 Cor. 15:26). God does not make a deal with death in order to accomplish His ends. In modern Christian culture, we make statements such as, "we will understand it better bye and bye" or that "God healed that person through death – they are better now". This implies that the God who sent Jesus to give us life and life more abundantly (John 10:10) uses his greatest enemy to bring about His intentions for His best-loved subjects (the children of men). If you are going to understand the implications of Enoch's life and translation as relating to you personally, you are going to have to clear up your thinking in this one area of religious ambiguity. Death is your enemy and Jesus came to give you eternal life that has a bearing, not only on the afterlife but also upon you own human mortality. In the gospel of John:

> [John 8:51 KJV] 51 Verily, verily, I say unto you, If a man keep my saying, he shall never see death.

Now at this point, many teachers and those who study the scriptures have waded out into uncharted waters and been lost in the riptides of false doctrine. We have no intention of scandalizing believers at this point or of breaching the bounds of our own orthodoxy. In other words, "listen to what I'm saying and what I'm not saying". If we hope to be sincere in our study of scripture we have to take off our religious glasses that explain away or rationalize through unbelief the contradiction between our experience and God's promises even in the universal concern of our own mortality and inevitable (?) death. Enoch was translated at age

365. God put 365 "fear nots" in the Bible. All fear arises from death, yet the unambiguous words of Jesus compel us not to fear death but to believe in Him.

Conclusion:

Let's look lastly at the story of Jesus and Lazarus. In John chapter 11, Jesus receives word that his friend Lazarus is sick. He lingers in his response and consequently Lazarus dies. Jesus shows up late to the situation and finds Martha grieving:

> *[John 11:21-26 KJV] 21 Then said Martha unto Jesus, Lord, if thou hadst been here, my brother had not died. 22 But I know, that even now, whatsoever thou wilt ask of God, God will give [it] thee. 23 Jesus saith unto her, Thy brother shall rise again.*

We often have the same response to our problems that Martha demonstrates in her greeting to Jesus. "IF" God had shown up in our situation then things might have been different. Perhaps we might frame it in a question to show our real frustration: "God where were you? Why did you leave me to suffer in my circumstance?"

The unbelief of the question betrays a conviction that it is possible for Jesus to be late. Jesus cannot be late. Jesus is God and Jesus created time and eternity. It is not possible for Him to be late and it is not possible for Him not to be anywhere and everywhere at any given moment – specifically locating Himself at the point of your need. Jesus ignores Martha's veiled accusation and ignores her religious platitude that she follows up with. He tells Martha bluntly "Your brother shall live…"

> *24 Martha saith unto him, I know that he shall rise again in the resurrection at the last day. 25 Jesus said unto her, I am the resurrection, and the life: he that believeth in me, though he were dead, yet shall he live: 26 And whosoever liveth and believeth in me shall never die. Believest thou this?*

Martha listens to Jesus' words without really hearing them. She leaves and tells Mary "the master calleth for thee…" In other words, she is frustrated. She tells Mary in effect "He is talking your language not mine – I have a funeral to arrange for…" Martha is overwhelmed at the enormity and finality of Lazarus death and like so many of us she relegates the pain and sorrow and ultimate closure of the situation to the last day. She is agreeing with Jesus but putting

Lazarus' resurrection off to "one day" and "some day".

Jesus doesn't let the matter go. He keeps talking. He is speaking from His NOW and He is compelling Martha to stay focused in the NOW and not give in to unbelief. Relegating answered prayer to some unaccountable "some day" is unbelief. Miracles happen in the now. Now is all that God has to give you. Past and Future are the perspectives of the sinful man and a consequence of the fall. God has no such limitation. He is everywhere present and always now. He is never late. He is never preoccupied. He never fails to be on task and on target at the point of your need EVEN WITH RESPECT TO YOUR OWN MORTALITY. Paul addressed the inconvenient truth of God's confrontation of our mortality with the following statements:

> *[1Th 4:16-18 KJV] 16 For the Lord himself shall descend from heaven with a shout, with the voice of the archangel, and with the trump of God: and the dead in Christ shall rise first: 17 Then we which are alive [and] remain shall be caught up together with them in the clouds, to meet the Lord in the air: and so shall we ever be with the Lord. 18 Wherefore comfort one another with these words.*

This is not an eschatological conclusion to this chapter. It is a personal one. When is this going to happen? When did it happen to Enoch or Elijah? If it happened to Enoch and Elijah why not us? Death is our enemy. There will be (if you believe the passage) a company of believers who are going to get that and understand that and look to God to receive a cancellation slip of their appointment with death.

Chapter Three

Walk Like Enoch Walked

Introduction: Walk Like Enoch Walked

In part one of our study, we reviewed the implications of the two Enochs of scripture. In Matt. 6:24 Jesus said no man serves two masters. In life, you will demonstrate one of two mandates – that of the kingdom or the domain of darkness. Enoch's name means "dedicated or consecrated". You will either live your life dedicated to self or dedicated to the Father – and there is no third alternative. In part two of our study, we saw that God cancelled Enoch's appointment with death. Heb. 9:27 tells us everyone has an appointment with death – but God cancelled Enoch and Elijah's appointment.

There are those who believe that the two witnesses of Rev. 11:1-7 will actually be Enoch and Elijah and they will therefore die and meet their appointment with the last enemy. Nowhere in scripture is this explicitly stated or even implied. It is simply a conjecture based on a rational argument. We can also point to those which are "alive and remain" in 1 Th. 4:17, as a significant number of people alive on the earth who at some point are going to have their appointment with death cancelled. We are all familiar with the scriptural theme of resurrection, and accept it in one form or another. In this continuation of our study, we will look at Enoch and what the Bible says about him to determine what, if anything, we can learn about his character and actions that may have contributed to his being chosen by God to go to heaven without going by way of death. Peter stated in Acts 10:34 that God is no respecter of persons, but He is a respecter of faith. Enoch and Elijah, we pointed out in our previous study, were not unique in their character. What God did for Enoch He may do for others. If we do with our faith what Enoch did with his faith, we may be eligible for the same experience.

Enoch, Methuselah and Human Longevity:

There is much information to be found about the life, character and experiences of Enoch. In this chapter, we will confine ourselves to what the Bible tells us about him. Again Enoch was the seventh from Adam, the son of Jared and the father of Methuselah. Methuselah was born to Enoch when he was 65 years of age and went on to be the longest lived man according to the Biblical record. It is interesting that Methuselah was the longest lived of the 10 antediluvian patriarchs, yet his father Enoch was the shortest lived. The fact that Methuselah died before reaching the age of 1000 is significant as well. God told Adam that in the day he would partake of the tree of the knowledge of good and evil he would die. Adam died 127 years before Noah at the age of 930. So, he didn't die in the 24 hour day that he ate of the forbidden tree. However, Peter declares (2 Peter 3:8) that a day with the Lord is 1000 years and 1000 years is as a day. Calculating by that measurement, Adam dying at the age of 930 did die in the day that he ate of the fruit as has every other man of the human race, including

Methuselah who did not live beyond 1000 years. We will come back to 2 Peter 3:8 later on in our studies of Enoch.

How Long was Man Designed to Live?

There are two Old Testament references to Enoch's walk with God. Firstly, in Gen. 5:22 we see he walked with God and begat Methuselah. That was his first accomplishment. Methuselah's name means "man of the dart". Names in scripture were not without signification. Psalm 127:1 says "as arrows in the hand of a mighty man so are the children of thy youth…" Enoch walked with God and fired Methuselah as an arrow out of his loins at a target? What target would that be? I believe he expected Methuselah to live out the day that Adam's sin denied him and subsequently denied every one of us. Methuselah lived 969 years. He died 31 years short of 1000.

If Adam and Eve had not sinned would they still be walking around on the earth? I believe that Enoch is an example of the fact that they would not. Just because man did not sin and therefore not die – does not mean that there would not even in the life of a sinless man be a departure from the earth. Rev. 12 describes a church caught up to the second heaven as a sun clothed woman. She then gives birth to a "man child" who is caught up to the third heaven and to the throne. 1 Thess. 4:15-17 describes a people caught up to heaven (therefore obviously not in a sin state) who go to heaven by circumventing death. Just because death is not involved does not mean there would not be a departure from the earth at some point as Enoch, Elijah, and the adjudicated church suggest. It is very possible that God may have designed mankind to live out a 1000 year day and be caught up to the third heaven as Enoch was.

Walk Like Enoch Walked:

[Gen 5:24 And Enoch walked with God: and he [was] not; for God took him.

Enoch walked with God and was not for God took him. What does this mean? What is it about Enoch walking with God that brought him to the place that he was translated? The word walk here is the Hebrew word "halak" meaning *to "go to, go toward, to traverse, to be wont (or prone) to haunt"*.

It also means to *walk continually* and to *be conversant* and to *bear the tale* of God. So, this is more than physically walking - it speaks of a lifestyle.

Where it implies to *walk continually* it speaks of consistency. We see the value of maintaining a constant and unswerving fidelity and intimacy with God over time. Young people as they grow older and live more than two or three decades will begin to discover aspects of life and trends of life and walking with God that produce fruit only after several decades have passed. Enoch was in his 4th century of life when he was translated. There are fruitfulness and blessing from God that won't be experienced or appreciated until many years have passed. Be patient. Stay consistent. Don't live for God one year and go back to the world the next.

The word "walk" there also means to "bear a tale". The scriptures speak against being a talebearer, but we aren't talking about idle gossip here. Enoch carried a message. He is quoted numerous times in the New Testament including by Jesus Himself which we will cover later – but Enoch carried a message, and God wants our lives to carry a message and not just be some random experience of a life lived in self-referral and narcissism.

My favorite part of this definition of the word for walk is that Enoch "haunted" God. The Merriam-Webster definition of haunt means to *visit often; to continually seek the company of; to habitually stay around* [a person, place or thing]. Enoch haunted God. Every time God turned around there was Enoch. What might that be like? When I was a young father, my oldest son just learning to talk would follow me around and tug on my pant leg. He would tug on my cuffs and say over and over "daddy, daddy, daddy…" I would be quite busy and about my day but he was persistent. He wouldn't go away. He didn't have anywhere else to be. He would not be distracted. He didn't need a break. I wasn't one of his priorities I WAS his priority. Finally, one day I reached down and picked him up by the straps of his overalls and said, "Why don't you just come with me today?"

This is exactly what God did with Enoch. Enoch *haunted* God. Every time God turned around – there was Enoch. He was persistent. He wouldn't go away. He didn't have anywhere else to be or anyone else he wanted to be with. He would not be distracted. He didn't need a break. He didn't separate between sacred and secular or between spiritual and natural. He said within his heart, "it's all the same" and would not relinquish his intimacy with God for anything. Finally, God

reached down and picked Enoch up like he did
Ezekiel when he picked him up by the lock of his
hair and showed him his glory.

"Why don't you just come with Me today,
Enoch?"

And Enoch walked with God for God took him.
His translation was not some capricious, cosmic
stunt God pulled off just to impress mankind.
This was an intimate transaction between Enoch
and his Maker, his Friend and his Father. In
terms of translation, Enoch set the standard for
what that looks like. What about Elijah? Elijah
was the man in 1 Kings 19:13 who wrapped his
face in his mantle when he talked to God. He was
a man of like passions as we are but his
relationship with God was one of intimacy and
authenticity.

Enoch Walked with God for God Took Him:

How old was Enoch when he was translated? He
was 365. What were the significant events in his
life before that? If you do the math, you will find

that Enoch was 308 years old when Adam died at the age of 930. That may or may not seem important until you realize that at the time that Adam died there was no other recorded death by natural causes. There were at least 2 murders by this time, probably more, but Adam's death of old age is the first verifiable death by natural causes.

What happens when someone dies in your family? You are called to the funeral. No doubt there was some funereal rite planned and carried out in behalf of Adam that Enoch would have been invited to. Being one of the junior patriarchs by age, he might have been responsible for some of the logistics of Adam's ceremony. He certainly would have viewed Adam's body after death. Imagine it. No one has seen a body dead by natural causes. Here around the body stands Seth, Enosh, Cainan, grandfather Mahalal and Jared, Enoch's father. Enoch is there as well. All patriarch's staring upon the stark consequences of Adam's disobedience. Staring at their own future. Looking upon what awaited them all. It was inevitable. Then deep down in Enoch's heart, there is a stirring and he resolves in his soul "not for me!"

How do we know that Enoch resolved at some point he would not go by way of death? If we can't prove it we are in danger of false doctrine and ungodly speculation. Consider what we covered earlier in this study about the meaning of Methuselah's name. Enoch seemingly saw the life of his son as an arrow fired at a target. By Methuselahs' long life we can deduce that it is very likely that Enoch's expectation was that his own son would outlive the curse brought on by Adam's sin.

Is this our only proof? It would be pretty thin conjecture if we didn't have another reference showing that translation was EXACTLY what Enoch had in mind. In the great faith chapter in Hebrews, we find the following verse:

> [Heb 11:5 KJV] 5 By faith Enoch was translated that he should not see death; and was not found, because God had translated him: for before his translation he had this testimony, that he pleased God.

Notice that Enoch was translated *by faith.* That means he put his mind upon it. He was hoping for it. He was expecting it to take place. Hebrews 11:1 tells us this about faith:

> [Heb 11:1 KJV] 1 Now faith is the substance of things hoped for, the evidence of things not seen.

The implication of this verse is that faith must be specific. You cannot adopt the attitude "God knows what I need – if he wants me to have it, he will give it to me…" There is no hope in that statement. There is only vague resignation. Faith is not about resignation or wishful thinking. Faith is specific and has an object in mind. In Enoch's case, he was expecting and believing in his walk with God to be translated. So we see his LOVE for God in his walk and his FAITH in God for translation. Faith works by love – and we see in Enoch's case the result.

Conclusion:

In Hebrews 11:5, we see in the simplest language that Enoch wasn't translated because of some mystical understanding he had that is not accessible to us. Neither was his translation initiated solely as an act of divine sovereignty because God had a point to prove or some cosmic stunt to pull off. Enoch's translation was initiated on Enoch's side of the transaction by his faith. We have no indication that God had any plans to translate Enoch. But we do know that Enoch had his faith upon translation – perhaps for a very long time. He was translated by faith. Not just religious faith but a faith that was working by love. Enoch walked with God. He haunted God. He had nowhere other to be in his life than with God. Enoch saw the results of sin in the death of Adam by natural causes. He hoped that his son Methuselah would fulfill the 1000 year day that no other patriarch had fulfilled in his lifespan.

The Bible promises that one day we will put on immortality. Will it be any different for us than it was for Enoch? Is God going to forego the requirement of faith and intimate relationship one day and just bring to heaven everyone who has signed a decision card and prayed the sinner's prayer? Or is, as in the case of Enoch, faith going to be involved? Is faith a requisite to overcome death? As one teacher has said, "faith comes by hearing" and "hearing by the word of God". If we don't preach immortality and believe for walking into our immortality, what makes us think we will ever experience it? What diverse believers call the rapture, the adjudication of the saints, putting on immortality, the manifestation of the sons of God – call it what you will, it is about a people walking with God and being not, for God will take them into a dispensation or experience that will exclude death as a means of going to the father. You cannot believe the scriptures and deny that one day this will take place. Not because God pushes some magic button and overlooks the requirements of faith and fidelity, but because a people have been raised up to boldly believe that for them, like Enoch, the last enemy (death must be put under foot).

Chapter Four

Talk Like Enoch Talked

Introduction: Talk Like Enoch Talked

Enoch did not pass down to approved canon, any books that we can revere as holy writ, however, there is one direct quote from Enoch in the books of Jude and 2 Peter and many veiled references to it by the New Testament writers and even Jesus Himself. The quote from Jude is:

> *[Jude 1:14-15 KJV] 14 And Enoch also, the seventh from Adam, prophesied of these, saying, Behold, the Lord cometh with ten thousands of his saints, 15 To execute judgment upon all, and to convince all that are ungodly among them of all their ungodly deeds which they have ungodly committed, and of all their hard [speeches] which ungodly sinners have spoken against him.*

The fact that Jude quotes the book of Enoch does not mean that the book of Enoch is, therefore, to be accepted on the level of the other canonical books. Paul quotes the Greek philosopher Epimenides in Titus 1:12, but that doesn't mean that the writings attributed to Epimenides are to be considered canonical. We answer these questions because many young zealots are anxious to find out some new insight that perhaps might be found in extra-biblical manuscripts that scholarship is aware of. Besides the book of Enoch, other manuscripts and ancient writings that get such attention include The Shepherd of Hermas, the Secret Sayings of Thomas, and other writings brought to light with the Dead Sea scrolls.

Does the Book of Enoch Belong in the Canon of Scripture:

No, the book of Enoch was not considered as canonical by the generations we look back on in history that were tasked with traversing that time when decisions were made about what is "bible" and what is not. What we know of the book of Enoch most commonly comes from a version put together in 1906 by Robert Henry Charles from 28 manuscripts of Enoch available to him at the time. In none of that collection of manuscripts do we find the quote that Jude used and attributed to Enoch. However in 1956, there was found among the Dead Sea Scrolls a book called "Enoch" that contains an almost direct correlating quote of Jude 14-15.

Regardless of the light that we can draw from the three distinct and primary versions of the Book of Enoch available, the one reliable truth we can look to is the endorsement of heaven to Enoch's words quoted from Jude in his epistle. We shall look at that and consider the remainder of the book of Enoch in its various forms to be interesting, a historical oddity but not holy writ. Having said that, however, it would be hard to deny that Jesus, the apostles and several centuries of early church development were greatly influenced by the book of Enoch, therefore, we do not lightly dismiss it, but put it in its proper, venerated place but not for it's infallibility that we would attribute to the canon of 66 accepted books.

Talk Like Enoch Talked – the Message of Enoch:

The message of Enoch will be drawn from the direct quote of Enoch in Jude (also in 2 Peter) and several veiled quotes we could make note of but will not for the sake of time. In the book of 2 Peter we find two quotes attributed by scholars to Enoch:

> *[2Pe 2:4 KJV] 4 For if God spared not the angels that sinned, but cast [them] down to hell, and delivered [them] into chains of darkness, to be reserved unto judgment;*
>
> *[2Pe 3:13 KJV] 13 Nevertheless we, according to his promise, look for new heavens and a new earth, wherein dwelleth righteousness.*

Again, our point is not to elevate purported writings of Enoch by connecting them with scripture, but to highlight passages where New Testament writers were influenced by manuscripts attributed to Enoch in their day, so much so, that they transferred them to what eventually became for us sacred scripture. Having done so, we can at least, with some reliability, attribute the quotes to Enoch and believe the Holy Spirit would not have given them to us as coming from Enoch unless they actually did – if you, in fact, believe the Bible is inspired, given by God and infallible.

From the 2 Peter references, we see that that the 2nd-century view regarding angels, and hell, and punishment of disobedient angels was influenced by writings of Enoch that are attributed *in Holy Scripture to Enoch.* Enoch also, from the reference of 2 Peter 3:13, believed and prophesied about an enduring earth where righteousness would dwell. What does this tell us about Enoch? Beginning with Methuselah and the message of his name given by Enoch – Enoch was preoccupied with what we call Eschatology or the study of end things. He was looking forward looking. He hoped to see his son live out the 1000 year day that Adam's sin condemns us all to die in. He was, according to Heb. 11:5, putting his faith on overcoming death. His translation took place just 57 years after the first recorded natural death so it is probable that the natural death of

Adam galvanized him to believe and appropriate by faith the opportunity to step from mortality to immortality without going by way of the grave.

Are We Skating on Dangerous Ground to Study Enoch?

If Enoch was translated by faith (therefore apparently putting his specific hope in being translated (e.g. Heb. 11:5 faith is the substance of *things hoped for*)) – are we wrong or on dangerous ground to put OUR faith on a translation experience? If Enoch, according to Hebrews 11:5, was translated by faith, then on what basis are those of 1 Thess. 4:17 going to be translated? Are we to put our faith on walking into immortality like Enoch did, or is the *parousia* (catching up) going to simply be a sovereign act of God as He is in the course of working out a timeline of scheduled end-time events? We would submit to you that if the *parousia* (catching up, rapture, adjudication of the saints, redemption of the purchased possession, body felt salvation, manifestation of the sons of God – whatever you want to call it) isn't a faith proposition, it would not please God to do so.

[Heb 11:6 KJV] 6 But without faith [it is] impossible to please [him]...

[Rom 14:23 KJV]... for whatsoever [is] not of faith is sin.

Faith is not faith unless it has a specific object in mind. To just blithely put our expectations on a vague acknowledgement of resurrection one day is not faith. Faith that is not now is not faith. Remember the facetious statement of Martha to Jesus when He declared to her that her brother Lazarus would live – and her response was a dismissive religious platitude:

[John 11:23-26 KJV] 23 Jesus saith unto her, Thy brother shall rise again. 24 Martha saith unto him, I know that he shall rise again in the resurrection at the last day. 25 Jesus said unto her, I am the resurrection, and the life: he that believeth in me, though he were dead, yet shall he live: 26 And whosoever liveth and believeth in me shall never die. Believest thou this?

Is it Wrong to Put Our Hope and Our Faith in a Never Die Expectation?

When Martha marginalized the words of Jesus with her religious banality, He directly challenged her with these words: "I am the resurrection and the life…" In other words, Jesus was saying, "stop relegating miracles you are having a hard time believing into a 'one-day; some-day' unlikelihood". He wanted her to believe that her brother's resurrection would not originate in an eschatological eventuality but that Lazarus resurrection would originate in the person of Jesus on that day at that moment.

What about your resurrection? Scholars might say that Jesus never intended for us to construe His conversation with Martha to apply to our own mortality. Yet, considering the stark simplicity of his words, what else are we to think?

> *[John 11:23-26 KJV] … 25 Jesus said unto her, I am the resurrection, and the life: he that believeth in me, though he were dead, yet shall he live: 26 And whosoever liveth and believeth in me shall never die. Believest thou this?*

Looking at this verse as a suggestion that resurrection and immortality are available to us as they were to Enoch is a tremendous challenge to our faith. Scholars and theologians would denounce us for even suggesting it. But the

words of Jesus couldn't be clearer –
"…whosoever liveth and believeth in me shall never die – BELIEVEST THOU THIS?" Most Christians, if they were honest, do not believe this and have no intention of believing it. They expect to go by way of the grave unless Jesus comes back and whisks them to glory through a process that requires nothing more of them than to sign a decision card for Jesus and be living as a Christian when he returns.

The Parousia will be a Faith Proposition or Not at All:

I would submit to you that those who participate in the parousia of 1 Thess. 4:17 will be those that, like Enoch in Heb. 11:5 will be able to say they were *translated by faith.* They will be those holding forth the specific hope by faith in God for the unlikely and improbable outcome of stepping into an immortal life as Enoch did and Elijah on the same basis. Is this blasphemy? Hebrews 13:8 says that Jesus is the same yesterday, today and forever. Is the opportunity to be translated only an Old Testament anomaly not available to us today? How can that be when Hebrews 8:6 insists that the New Testament economy of God is established on a better covenant by the blood of the son of God and not the imperfect covenant based on the blood of bulls and goats in the Old Testament? The bandwidth of legitimate New Covenant expectations must include the whole of the Old Testament gifts and graces and go beyond it by the measure of the comparison of the excellency of the shed blood of Christ to the shed blood of animal sacrifice.

The inclusive message of the gospel inextricably included the hope of immortality as Jesus defines it in John chapter 11 in his conversation with Martha. In 2 Tim. 1:10, Paul declares that the preciousness of the gospel includes the fact that it brings "… life and immortality to light *through* the gospel." How will immortality come? Through the gospel. Coming through a sovereign act that does not involve volition or cooperation on our part does not fit what Paul is stating. If it comes through the gospel, it must involve a message received, believed and acted upon or it falls inert at our feet. Therefore, it must be preached. Immortality and life as defined by the words of Jesus and declared by Paul must be preached in order to be believed and believed in order to be appropriated.

> [Rom 10:14 KJV] 14 How then shall they call on him in whom they have not believed? and

> *how shall they believe in him of whom they*
> *have not heard? and how shall they hear*
> *without a preacher?*

Therefore, it is incumbent upon us who claim to preach the gospel to include this theme of resurrection by faith in our preaching.

Conclusion:

Death is not a friend, death is your enemy (1 Co. 15:26). God does not need and God does not use His enemies to achieve an end He intends for His friends:

> *[Jas 1:17 KJV] 17 Every good gift and every*
> *perfect gift is from above and cometh down*
> *from the Father of lights, with whom is no*
> *variableness, neither shadow of turning.*

Paul said this:

> *[1Ti 6:16 KJV] 16 Who only [Jesus] hath*
> *immortality, dwelling in the light which no*
> *man can approach unto; whom no man hath*

seen, nor can see: to whom [be] honour and
power everlasting. Amen.

Death is not the doorman to immortality. Only Jesus is the door to immortality. He does not need the services of death to make you immortal. The process by which faith brings you to the crises experience of immortality is a matter of a faith transaction. You are hoping for immortality, expecting immortality and believing for immortality as Enoch evidently did and, in fact, received.

> *[1Co 15:53, 55-58 KJV] 53 For this corruptible must put on incorruption, and this mortal [must] put on immortality. ... 55 O death, where [is] thy sting? O grave, where [is] thy victory? 56 The sting of death [is] sin; and the strength of sin [is] the law. 57 But thanks [be] to God, which giveth us the victory through our Lord Jesus Christ. 58 Therefore, my beloved brethren, be ye stedfast, unmoveable, always abounding in the work of the Lord, forasmuch as ye know that your labour is not in vain in the Lord.*

The assertions of 1 Thess. 4:17, regarding those which are alive and remain who are caught up to immortality, are far more than the description of an eschatological event. The experience described in 1 Thess. 4:17 has much in common with those 120 that were gathered in the upper room in Acts waiting on the promise of the Father. They received the promise that was given because they chose to believe and to hold out the expectation of an immediate manifestation. Likewise, those that lay hold on the 1 Thess. 4:17 experience will be those choosing to believe and to hold out an expectation to one day both individually and corporately walk into immortality by Christ Jesus.

Chapter Five

Do We Have all that God has for Us?

Introduction: Do We Have all that God Has For us?

In 1900, Charles Parham gathered 40 students together in Topeka, Kansas to answer the question, "is the baptism of the Holy Ghost for us today?" On New Year's Eve, that question was answered and all of Christianity was changed from that moment. Do we have all that God has for us? We have experienced the new birth. Millions claim to have received the baptism of the Holy Ghost with the evidence of speaking in other tongues. Is that it in terms of personal experiences available to the believer this side of a dispensational shift into the rarified atmosphere of eschatological speculation? Is there any Biblical indication that something is yet out there for us if we are willing to have the bold spirit of inquiry demonstrated by Parham and the Topeka students, in the beginning, days of 1900?

For many up until the time of the Great Awakening, the idea of a personal experience with God was the purview of mystics and monastics. A Proper relationship with God for 100's of years was understood in the context of being rightly related to the institutions of church, the liturgy and the local parish. Then George Whitfield, Jonathan Edwards and others came on the scene advocating not only a religion you could feel but a God that could be experienced personally. The God of the Great Awakening was not arbitrated by the institutions of the church, but took up residence in the human heart on a case by case individual basis. The concept of the New Birth began to be common place in the religious experience of the Western World. Out of the Great Awakening came the Evangelical Movement, and in a few generations, anything outside the Evangelic Movement was labeled as the nominal or "in name only" institution of Christianity.

Glimmerings of Glory this Side of Heaven:

To be sure, there had been glimmerings of unique and deeply personal experiences in God evidenced in movements like the Moravians, the Waldenses, the Quakers and the Puritans that captured our imagination and pointed us to something more in God. Over the course of the 500 years since the reformation under Martin Luther and now the late invention of the Pentecostal movement, people have pretty much felt as though in the fullness of the Spirit was contained the whole of personal experiences with God available on this side of heaven. The nagging question remains, however, and is open to Biblical inquiry: Do we have it all? Do we have every personal, universal experience available to the believer on this side of heaven?

This is more than just the vain question of a bored church polity looking for some new experience to titillate religious sentiments. This spirit of inquiry inflamed the people who listened to the words of John the Baptist from the shores of the Jordan. The great revivals in the last 500 years from Martin Luther to the Toronto Outpouring have been born of the quest for more of God – for all of God that can be had this side of our mortality.

The New Birth and the Baptism of the Holy Spirit:

Far from being universally accepted and sought after, the idea of a "New Birth" is generally the convention of a handful of Christian movements such as Fundamentalism and Evangelicalism. Generally, the New Birth so termed is seen as the rite of initiation into the ranks of Christianity both from an ecclesiastical perspective and as a matter of faith from God's point of view as well. According to the Encyclopedia of World Religions, the unique character of the idea of a New Birth is that relationship to God then becomes a personal and individual experience and pursuit as contrasted from the institutional and liturgical constructs of the historical churches. Catholicism historically has viewed the explicit connection to Christ as being implied by proper attachment and immersion into the institution of the Church of Rome while not rejecting altogether the idea of further and personal experience such as the New Birth. The last two Popes have somewhat embraced the idea of the New Birth in the emphasis styled by Pope John Paul II as the "New Evangelization" that emphasizes "fullness of faith" to include deeply personal and experiential knowledge of Christ within the parameters of Catholic faith and the Eucharist.

The Lutheran and Anglican churches embrace, at least in theory and stated theology, an acknowledgment of the necessity of renewal and regeneration by the Holy Spirit. The Reformed Churches reject the idea of the New Birth altogether. Methodism and other Evangelical churches embrace the idea of the New Birth unequivocally as a personal experience and ongoing relationship with God not arbited or requiring liturgical or ecclesiastical validation through the Eucharist or various liturgies.

The Baptism of the Holy Spirit, arising from the scriptural precedent of the events of Acts chapter 2 is a pervasive belief throughout most Christian movements and denominations to a lesser or greater degree. The difference of beliefs regarding the Holy Spirit centers on the modality of receiving it and the controversial aspects of speaking in other tongues and accompanying gifts and graces such as the 9 gifts of the Spirit mentioned in 1 Cor. 12. The more personal and intense the proposed experience is – the more controversial and less commonly held it becomes in terms of belief and acceptance among the institutions of Christianity.

Is There Another Baptism?

The teachings of John the Baptist include references enjoined by Fundamentalists and Evangelicals relating to the New Birth and, less commonly, the Baptism of the Holy Spirit as a personal and "crises" occurrence appropriated by faith and experienced in a very individual and intimate spiritual epiphany. In reading the scriptures referring to John's teaching, we can see where the idea of New Birth and the Baptism of the Holy Spirit are referred to, but is there something more?

> [Mat 3:11 KJV] 11 I indeed baptize you with water unto repentance: but he that cometh after me is mightier than I, whose shoes I am not worthy to bear: he shall baptize you with the Holy Ghost, and [with] fire:

A deconstruction of the language of Matt. 3:11 reveals references to the New Birth, to the Baptism of the Holy Spirit – and something more perhaps in those three words "…and with fire". There is not agreement on this of course, as various groups presume that the experience they embrace (say the New Birth for instance) is the only experience referenced in the passage and that the mention of "baptism of Spirit" and "with fire" is simply a poetic extension of a description of the New Birth. In other words, they contend when you get born again you receive all that God has for you as defined by Mat. 3:11

Pentecostals and Charismatics take things a bit further suggesting and, in fact, insisting there is a second definitive experience from the New Birth explicitly identified in the wording "he shall baptize you with the Holy Ghost" as referencing the experience of receiving the gift of tongues or glossolalia. One proof text Pentecostal theology provides a distinction between the New Birth and the Holy Spirit baptism, is found in Acts 19:2:

> *[Act 19:2 KJV] 2 He said unto them, Have ye received the Holy Ghost since ye believed? And they said unto him, We have not so much as heard whether there be any Holy Ghost.*

The believers, in Acts 19:2, are held to be born again but in need of (according to Paul) the second experience of receiving the Baptism of the Holy Ghost with evidence of speaking in other tongues. However, it must be noted that Pentecostal and Charismatic believers make the assumption that when the baptism of the Holy Ghost comes it is "the Holy Ghost and Fire" thence, concluding NOW we have it all. Thus, they reject the thinking of non-Pentecostals that the New Birth is a universal experience including "baptism of the Holy Ghost and fire", insisting that the Baptism of the Holy Ghost is separate from the New Birth. However, they presume, without pause, that the Baptism of the Holy Ghost "and fire" is merely a poetic extension of the language describing what happens when one receives the initial gift of glossolalia.

The Mistaken Thinking of Pentecostals and Charismatics:

Do we not make the same mistake – commit the same error as the cessationists who were so quick to believe there was nothing more in God than what they were prepared to believe and experience beyond the two accepted experiences of New Birth and the Baptism of the Holy Ghost? From an objective analysis of the teaching of John, the Baptism points to not two but three distinct experiences: 1.) Salvation; 2.) Holy Spirit Baptism; 3.) Something as yet universally understood – the "and with fire" Baptism. Parham, in 1900, rightly and bravely posed the question to his students, "do we have the Baptism of the Holy Spirit as part of our New Birth or is there something more?" Could we (and perhaps should) pose the same question regarding the Baptism of Fire? Do we have the Baptism of Fire as part of the Baptism of the Holy Ghost or is there something more? Is there a personal, experiential experience of "Fire Baptism" that is generally not in evidence, yet clearly pointed to in the scriptures? Having posed the question, the remainder of this study will make some suggestions:

Indicators of a Third and Definite Experience of Fire Baptism Available to Us:

Under the law, the people were required to appear "three times before the Lord".

[Exo 23:17 KJV] 17 Three times in the year all

thy males shall appear before the Lord GOD.

There are three feasts that were celebrated –
Passover (salvation); Pentecost (Spirit baptism)
and Tabernacles.

There are actually three feasts of the seventh
month grouped together under the title of the
feast of tabernacles. They are the feast of
trumpets, the day of atonement and the actual
feast of tabernacles. The seven feasts in order are:

Passover (including Unleavened Bread and First
Fruits)
Pentecost (standing alone)
Trumpets (including Atonement and
Tabernacles.).

These feasts correspond in Evangelical /
Pentecostal theology to Salvation (or the New
Birth), the baptism of the Holy Ghost and for the
purposes of this inquiry - the baptism of fire (or
putting on of immortality, more commonly
known as the rapture of the church).

Passover is a metaphor for the New Birth.
Pentecost pre-shadows the Baptism of the Holy
Ghost. Most Pentecostal and Evangelical
theologians would agree with this more or less.
However, their system of thought breaks down

when referring to the Baptism of Fire as either 1.) Being inclusive of the Baptism of the Holy Spirit or, 2.) Actually referring to the rigors of the suffering and judgments brought on the world during the so-called "Great Tribulation".

We would contend that if the Passover points to a personal experience available to the believer and that Pentecost points to an experience available to the believer, then it follows that Tabernacles likewise points to an experience available to the believer – one that is not generally known or experienced except, perhaps historically, by Enoch and Elijah in full and the believers at Pentecost in part when tongues of fire appeared on their heads.

Passover speaks of regeneration of the Spirit. Pentecost points to the fullness of the Spirit in one's soul. Tabernacles addresses the only part of us left that has yet to experience transformation – that of our physical bodies. It speaks of moving from mortality to immortality. Remember the New Testament teaches we are the temple of God. One day there will be a people on the earth who will walk into immortality by the presence of God.

The scriptures teach that we are the temple where God chooses to dwell. If you look at the dimensions of the tabernacle in the wilderness and the temple of Solomon, you will see prefigured there not only a three-fold experience of salvation but also, you will see an implied timely pointing to our day as the day when man will walk into immortality through faith in Christ Jesus. This corresponds to the three promised experiences in God – salvation, baptism in the Holy Ghost and the Baptism of fire which was prefigured in the law as the three great feasts of Passover, Pentecost and Tabernacles. Thus, in the temple dimensions, we have the scope of salvation and the timeline of God's purposes from Eden until now. This all points to the day we live in as a time when the temple God has been building into man coming to its completion in our season in history.

What is tabernacles? In salvation, the human spirit is born again. In the baptism of the Holy Ghost, the mind is immersed in God's spirit (James 3:8). What about tabernacles? What is left? The redemption of the body – something physical in terms of transformation and putting on immortality for our bodies are the temple/tabernacle of God (1 Cor. 3:17). Now theologians in or out of the Evangelical movement don't have a problem with immortality at some point. The controversy arises in determining when and how that immortality will be experienced. Most theologians simply relegate the resurrection and immortality of the body as a one-day, some-day proposition as Martha did when she marginalized Jesus' statements regarding the impending resurrection of Lazarus (covered previously in this study).

What Would the Baptism of Fire Look Like?

Is there any example of the Baptism of Fire that might manifest or have an effect on the human body?

> *[Mat 17:2 KJV] 2 And [Jesus] was transfigured before them: and his face did shine as the sun, and his raiment was white as the light.*

Jesus went up on the mount with Peter, James and John and they saw Him go through a marvelous and stupefying transformation. It is interesting that the next thing that happens is Peter making a reference to the Feast of Tabernacles:

> *[Mat 17:4 KJV] 4 Then answered Peter, and said unto Jesus, Lord, it is good for us to be here: if thou wilt, let us make here three tabernacles; one for thee, and one for Moses,*

and one for Elias.

Luke 9:3 goes on to point out after Peter says this "… not knowing what he said…" But just because Peter doesn't know what he was saying doesn't mean he wasn't ON TO SOMETHING!

Three Feasts – Three Baptisms:

There are three feasts and three baptisms. The first two feasts and baptisms point directly to a personal, intimate spiritual experience impacting the spirit man and the soul (mind, will, emotions). Certainly it follows that there is a 3rd baptism?

Some call this the rapture, the adjudication of the saints, the redemption of the purchased possession, body-felt salvation, putting on immortality, but whatever it is or is not as modeled by Jesus in the transfiguration, it doesn't take us anywhere out of the earth, and after receiving it, no one will necessarily physically notice it (Matt. 17:9,19). When Jesus came down from the mountain, he encounters his men struggling to cast out a demon. He doesn't look any different to them and he strictly commanded

Peter, James and John not to tell anyone what they had seen happen to them. What was the point if it wasn't that Jesus brought them as witnesses to see exactly what John the Baptist suggested in his preaching would be available to all believers including you and me – a literal baptism of fire?

Is this the rapture? Is this the manifestation of the sons of God? Most theologians don't make the connection here because they see events such as the parousia and some egalitarian event that will include all believers in a mopping up operation as God prepares the earth for judgment. Our suggestion is that the generality with which the rapture is viewed has overlooked the intense and highly personal nature of a baptism of fire that the gospels plainly allude to. Whatever the rapture is – there is that aspect of it that will be personal, intimate and involve faith to receive just like salvation and baptism of the Spirit (Heb. 11:5).

Conclusion:

The baptism of the Holy Spirit, in the first century, initially came to a people who were seeking and setting themselves aside – suspending business as usual. They had been prepared by the preaching of Jesus and His instruction to go and tarry. Parham also no doubt prepared his little flock with many teachings before they set themselves to receive this experience on New Year's eve 1900. In this teaching regarding Enoch and specifically the Baptism of Fire in this concluding chapter, we are not attempting to conjure up some contrived religious phantasy invoked by some spiritual frenzy. What we are suggesting is that any honest inquiry into the scriptures should convince us that we don't "have it all yet". You can go where Enoch went. One day if 1 Thess. 4:17 is to be believed – an entire people or company of people will, in fact, experience this. If not now then when? The Day of Pentecost came on a day like any other day. After the events that took place then the sovereign outpouring became an everyday occurrence imparted by faith to the uninitiated by those who had experienced it. There are exciting things ahead for the people of God – if we are willing to humble ourselves to our need of a greater experience in God than we have appropriated.

Made in the USA
Monee, IL
07 January 2021